THE 50 STATES
FACT BOOK

Creative Media Applications, Inc.
Author: Michael Teitelbaum
Editor: Matt Levine
Copyeditor: Laurie Lieb
Interior Production: Alan Barnett

Reader's
Digest
Children's Books®

Pleasantville, New York • Montréal, Québec • Bath, United Kingdom

ALABAMA The Yellowhammer State

★
Montgomery

The Spanish arrived in Alabama in 1519, but the first permanent colony was set up there by the French in 1702. The United States and Spain gained control after the Revolutionary War (1775–83). The Confederacy was formed in Montgomery in 1861. In 1881, at the Tuskegee Institute, George Washington Carver did his famous agricultural research on peanuts. In the 1950s and 1960s, Alabama was the site of several key actions in the civil rights movement, including the Montgomery bus boycott in 1955–56 and the Freedom March from Selma to Montgomery in 1965. Today, Birmingham is known for its famous medical center.

State Stats

Abbreviation: AL

Area: 53,423 square miles (138,366 km²)

Total Population (2000 Census): 4,447,100

Capital: Montgomery

Date of Statehood: Became the 22nd state on December 14, 1819

Largest Cities (by population): Birmingham, Montgomery, Mobile, Huntsville, Tuscaloosa, Hoover

Flower: Camellia

Tree: Southern longleaf pine

Bird: Yellowhammer

State Motto: "We Dare Defend Our Rights"

Economy:
Agriculture – Cattle, cotton, nursery stock, peanuts, poultry and eggs, soybeans
Industry – Lumber and wood products, mining, paper products, rubber and plastic products

Famous Alabamians

Henry Louis (Hank) Aaron
baseball player

Tallulah Bankhead
actress

Lionel Hampton
jazz musician

Harper Lee
author

Joe Louis
boxer

Rosa Parks
civil rights activist

George Wallace
governor of Alabama

Rosa Parks Museum Car Exhibit

Fun Facts

- In 1886 Montgomery unveiled the world's first electric trolley system.

- Workers in Alabama built the rocket that put the first people on the moon.

- The highest point in Alabama is Cheaha Mountain, rising to 2,405 feet (733 m).

- In the 1950s, a prehistoric man's skeleton was found in Russell Cave, near Bridgeport.

- In 1902, in Montgomery, Dr. Luther Leonidas Hill performed open-heart surgery – the first surgery of this type done in the Western Hemisphere.

- The state of Alabama gets its name from the Native American Creek language. It translates as "tribal town."

State Flag

Juneau

Russian naval Captain Alexei Chirikov and his Danish partner, explorer Vitus Bering, landed in Alaska in 1741. They found a native population consisting of Eskimos, Aleuts, and other Native Americans. In 1867, U.S. Secretary of State William Seward bought the land from the Russians for $7.2 million. An 1880 census reported a population of 33,426 (all but 430 were natives.) The gold rush of 1898 brought an additional 30,000 people to Alaska almost all at once. In 1968, oil and natural gas were discovered in Prudhoe Bay. The oil now moves along the Trans-Alaska Pipeline for use throughout the United States. The pipeline was completed in 1977.

State Stats

Abbreviation: AK

Area: 656,425 square miles (1,700,141 km²)

Total Population (2000 Census): 626,932

Capital: Juneau

Date of Statehood: Became the 49th state on January 3, 1959

Largest Cities (by population): Anchorage, Juneau, Fairbanks, Sitka, Ketchikan, Kenai

Flower: Forget-me-not

Tree: Sitka spruce

Bird: Willow ptarmigan

State Motto: "North to the Future"

Economy:
Agriculture – Dairy products, livestock, nursery stock, seafood, vegetables
Industry – Food processing, gold and other mining, lumber and wood products, petroleum and natural gas, tourism

Famous Alaskans

Margaret Elizabeth Bell
author

William A. Egan
first governor of Alaska

Jewel
pop singer

Joe Juneau
prospector

Sydney Lawrence
painter

Hilary Lindh
Olympic skier

John Muir
naturalist

Glacier Bay

Fun Facts

- Benny Benson designed Alaska's state flag at the age of thirteen.

- Many Americans, believing the U.S. acquisition of Alaska to be a mistake, called the purchase "Seward's Folly."

- Seward paid just two cents an acre (0.4 ha) for Alaska.

- In 1943, the Aleutian Islands were invaded by Japan. This was the first battle fought in America since the Civil War (1861–65).

- Twenty-five percent of the oil that is produced in the United States comes from Alaska.

- Up to 88,000 barrels of oil per hour are moved a distance of 800 miles (1,287 km) along the Trans-Alaska Pipeline.

3

ARIZONA — The Grand Canyon State

★ Phoenix

In 1539, Marcos de Niza, a Spanish Franciscan friar, became the first European to enter Arizona. He was searching for the legendary Seven Cities of Gold. Early Spanish colonization was mostly for missionary purposes. After the Mexican-American War (1846–48), most of the Arizona Territory became part of the United States. Arizona's history is filled with legends of the Old West, and Tombstone is the site of the West's most famous shootout—the gunfight at the OK Corral. Arizona also contains one of the most spectacular natural wonders in the world—the Grand Canyon.

State Stats

Abbreviation: AZ

Area: 114,006 square miles (295,275 km²)

Total Population (2000 Census): 5,130,632

Capital: Phoenix

Date of Statehood: Became the 48th state on February 14, 1912

Largest Cities (by population): Phoenix, Tucson, Mesa, Glendale, Scottsdale, Chandler

Flower: Saguaro cactus blossom

Tree: Yellow palo verde

Bird: Cactus wren

State Motto: "God Enriches"

Economy:
Agriculture – Cattle, cotton, dairy products, hay, lettuce, nursery stock
Industry – Copper and other mining, electrical components and equipment, food processing, printing and publishing, tourism

Famous Arizonans

Lynda Carter
actress

Cesar Chavez
labor leader

Geronimo
Apache chief

Barry Goldwater
U.S. senator

Charles Mingus
jazz musician

Linda Ronstadt
pop singer

Kerri Strug
Olympic gymnast

The Grand Canyon at Sunset

Fun Facts

- More copper is produced in Arizona than in any other state.

- Arizona actually has official state neckwear—the bola tie.

- Arizona was connected to the eastern part of the United States in 1926 by the completion of the Southern Pacific Railroad.

- The original London Bridge was rebuilt in Lake Havasu City after being shipped from England stone by stone.

- The oldest Native American settlement in the United States is Oraibi in Arizona, which was founded by the Hopi.

- The Kitt Peak National Observatory in Sells is home to the world's largest solar telescope.

ARKANSAS The Natural State

State Flag

★
Little Rock

The French were the first European settlers in Arkansas, establishing the Arkansas Post colony in 1686. In 1803, the area that formed Arkansas was acquired by the United States as part of the Louisiana Purchase. In 1819, Arkansas broke away from Missouri to become a separate territory. The next few decades were marked by the growth of the cotton industry. Arkansas joined the Confederacy in 1861, but the northern parts were soon occupied by Union troops. Today, the food and lumber industries are Arkansas's biggest, and the state has the nation's only active diamond mine!

State Stats

Abbreviation: AR

Area: 53,182 square miles (137,741 km²)

Total Population (2000 Census): 2,673,400

Capital: Little Rock

Date of Statehood: Became the 25th state on June 15, 1836

Largest Cities (by population): Little Rock, Fort Smith, Fayetteville, North Little Rock, Jonesboro, Pine Bluff

Flower: Apple blossom

Tree: Pine (loblolly and shortleaf)

Bird: Mockingbird

State Motto: "The People Rule"

Economy:
Agriculture — Cattle, cotton, milk, poultry and eggs, rice, soybeans
Industry — Electrical equipment, fabricated metal products, food processing, machinery, paper products

Famous Arkansans

Maya Angelou
author, poet

Daisy Bates
civil rights activist

Helen Gurley Brown
magazine editor

Johnny Cash
country and western musician

William Jefferson Clinton
42nd president of the United States

Jay Hanna "Dizzy" Dean
baseball player

Mary Steenburgen
actress

Mount Magazine State Park

Fun Facts

- More than 9,700 miles (15,607 km) of streams and rivers can be found in Arkansas.

- Arkansas took its name from a French translation of the Sioux word *acansa,* which means "downstream place."

- Since the 1830s, people such as Franklin Roosevelt, Babe Ruth, and Al Capone have enjoyed Hot Springs National Park.

- At the Crater of Diamonds State Park, tourists search for many precious gems.

- The oldest national forest in the southern United States is Arkansas's Ouachita National Forest.

- Each year, in Stuttgart, people gather for the World's Championship Duck Calling Contest.

CALIFORNIA The Golden State

★ Sacramento

The first Spanish settlement in California was established in 1769. California became part of the United States in 1847, when Mexico surrendered the territory as a result of the Mexican-American War. The next year, gold was discovered at Sutter's Mill, and the resulting gold rush brought 40,000 prospectors into the state. It also opened the door to mass immigration, mostly from Asia. California is well known for Hollywood, the capital of the U.S. movie industry. The state also boasts both the lowest point and the highest point in the lower 48 states — Death Valley, 282 feet (86 m) below sea level, and Mount Whitney, 14,491 feet (4,417 m) high.

State Stats

Abbreviation: CA

Area: 163,707 square miles (424,001 km²)

Total Population (2000 Census): 33,871,648

Capital: Sacramento

Date of Statehood: Became the 31st state on September 9, 1850

Largest Cities (by population): Los Angeles, San Diego, San Jose, San Francisco, Long Beach, Fresno

Flower: California poppy

Tree: Redwood

Bird: California valley quail

State Motto: "Eureka!" ("I Have Found It!")

Economy:
Agriculture — Cattle, dairy products, fruits and nuts, nursery stock, vegetables, wine
Industry — Aerospace, computers and computer software, electrical components and equipment, film production, food processing, petroleum, tourism

Famous Californians

Shirley Temple Black
actress, U.S. ambassador

Julia Child
chef, television personality

Joe DiMaggio
baseball player

Isadora Duncan
dancer

Richard M. Nixon
37th president of the United States

Sally K. Ride
astronaut

John Steinbeck
author

Cable Car in San Francisco

Fun Facts

- San Bernardino County is the largest county in the United States, at almost 3 million acres (1.2 million ha).

- In Death Valley, the summer temperature goes higher than 115° F (46° C).

- On April 2, 1902, Los Angeles became the site of the first movie theater in the United States.

- The bristlecone pine is the oldest living species of tree at 4,600 years old. These trees can be found in the Inyo National Forest.

- One out of every eight people living in the United States lives in California.

- California produces more than 300,000 tons (272,000 mt) of grapes every year.

COLORADO The Centennial State

State Flag

★
Denver

Colorado was first claimed for Spain in 1706. The United States obtained the eastern part of the territory as part of the Louisiana Purchase in 1803. The central portion of Colorado was acquired in 1845, when Texas became a state, and the western part was added in 1848 as a result of the Mexican-American War. The state is famous for the Rocky Mountains, which tower at heights of 10,000 feet (3,048 m). Beautiful scenery and tall mountains make Colorado a prime tourist destination, and it boasts some of the best skiing in the United States. Rocky Mountain National Park is one of the state's most popular attractions.

State Stats

Abbreviation: CO

Area: 104,100 square miles (269,619 km²)

Total Population (2000 Census): 4,301,261

Capital: Denver

Date of Statehood: Became the 38th state on August 1, 1876

Largest Cities (by population): Denver, Colorado Springs, Aurora, Lakewood, Fort Collins, Pueblo

Flower: Rocky Mountain columbine

Tree: Blue spruce

Bird: Lark bunting

State Motto: "Nothing Without Providence"

Economy:
Agriculture — Cattle, corn, dairy products, hay, wheat
Industry — Chemical products, food processing, gold and other mining, machinery, scientific instruments, tourism, transportation equipment

Famous Coloradoans

Tim Allen
actor

M. Scott Carpenter
astronaut

Mary Coyle Chase
playwright

Eugene Fodor
violinist

Ruth Handler
inventor

Ouray
Ute chief

Florence Rena Sabin
medical researcher

Skier Enjoys the Colorado Mountains

Fun Facts

- More than one-third of the land in Colorado is owned by the U.S. government.

- At 1,053 feet (321 m), the Royal Gorge Bridge over the Arkansas River is the highest suspension bridge in the world.

- There are 222 state wildlife areas in Colorado.

- The longest street in America is Colfax Avenue, in Denver.

- If you climb thirteen steps up the state capitol building in Denver, you will be exactly one mile (1.6 km) above sea level.

- After experiencing the breathtaking view from Pikes Peak, Katherine Lee Bates wrote the song "America the Beautiful."

CONNECTICUT The Constitution State

Hartford

In 1633, the Dutch built a trading post near what is Hartford today, but they soon lost control of the area to the English, who colonized it. Later, Connecticut played a major role in the Revolutionary War, serving as the Continental Army's main supplier of weapons. Sometimes called "the Arsenal of the Nation," Connecticut became one of the most industrialized states in the United States. It also boasts the oldest newspaper still being published – *The Hartford Courant*, which was founded in 1764. Connecticut's 250-mile (420-km) shoreline along Long Island Sound is a popular tourist resort, and Yale University in New Haven is one of the nation's finest schools.

State Stats

Abbreviation: CT

Area: 5,544 square miles (14,359 km²)

Total Population (2000 Census): 3,405,565

Capital: Hartford

Date of Statehood: Became the fifth state on January 9, 1788

Largest Cities (by population): Bridgeport, New Haven, Hartford, Stamford, Waterbury, Norwalk

Flower: Mountain laurel

Tree: White oak

Bird: Robin

State Motto: "He Who Transplanted Still Sustains"

Economy:
Agriculture – Cattle, dairy products, eggs, nursery stock
Industry – Chemical products, electrical equipment, fabricated metal products, machinery, scientific instruments, transportation equipment

Famous Connecticutians

Ethan Allen
Revolutionary War hero

P. T. Barnum
circus promoter and showman

Eileen Farrell
opera singer

Katharine Hepburn
actress

Annie Leibovitz
photographer

Benjamin Spock
pediatrician

Harriet Beecher Stowe
author

Amistad Replica at Mystic, Connecticut

Fun Facts

- The first telephone book was published in New Haven in 1878. It had 50 names in it.

- In 1954, the first nuclear-powered submarine, the USS *Nautilus*, was built in Groton.

- Connecticut was the first state in the United States to enact a law regarding automobiles. The 1901 law set the speed limit at 12 miles (19.3 km) per hour.

- Lollipops were first sold in New Haven in 1908.

- The first steel mill in the United States opened in 1728 in Simsbury.

- In 1917, the first golf tournament in Connecticut open only to women took place in the town of Waterbury.

DELAWARE The First State

★ Dover

Henry Hudson was the first European to discover Delaware in 1609. The colony of Delaware was settled by the Dutch, then claimed by the Swedish. It was then taken over by the Dutch again and finally claimed by the English in 1664. Although associated with the territory of Pennsylvania early on, during the Revolutionary War, Delaware fought as its own state. An 1802 gunpowder mill near Wilmington was the beginning of Delaware's large chemical industry, which, along with the food-canning industry, still dominates the state's economy.

State Stats

Abbreviation: DE

Area: 2,489 square miles (6,447 km²)

Total Population (2000 Census): 783,600

Capital: Dover

Date of Statehood: Became the first state on December 7, 1787

Largest Cities (by population): Wilmington, Dover, Newark, Milford, Seaford, Middletown

Flower: Peach blossom

Tree: American holly

Bird: Blue hen chicken

State Motto: "Liberty and Independence"

Economy:
Agriculture – Corn, dairy products, nursery stock, poultry, soybeans
Industry – Chemical products, food processing, paper products, printing and publishing, rubber and plastic products, scientific instruments

Famous Delawareans

Valerie Bertinelli
actress

Robert Montgomery Bird
playwright, author

Annie Jump Cannon
astronomer

E. I. DuPont
industrialist

Henry Heimlich
surgeon, inventor

Ruth Ann Minner
governor of Delaware

George Read
signer of the Declaration of Independence

Kalmar Nyckel, the Tall Ship of Delaware

Fun Facts

- Delaware has the distinction of being the first state to ratify the U.S. Constitution.

- In 1831, the first scheduled steam railroad in the United States started service in New Castle.

- Part of the small town of Delmar is in Delaware and part of it is in Maryland.

- The first log cabins in America were built in Delaware by Finnish settlers in the 1600s.

- Nylon was first created at the DuPont Labs in Seaford.

- In May, horseshoe crabs can be seen all along the Delaware shoreline. This type of crab has been around for millions of years.

FLORIDA The Sunshine State

Tallahassee ★

In 1513, Spanish explorer Juan Ponce de León was searching for the fountain of youth. Instead, he found Florida. Florida was held by Spain, then England, then Spain again until it was sold to the United States in 1819. The first half of the 18th century was marked by a long war with the Seminole people. In the early 20th century, Florida's beautiful weather and coastline became attractive to the tourist industry. Today, tourists flock to the state for the beaches, theme parks, and other attractions, such as the Kennedy Space Center and St. Augustine, the oldest permanent city in the United States.

State Stats

Abbreviation: FL

Area: 65,758 square miles (170,313 km²)

Total Population (2000 Census): 15,982,378

Capital: Tallahassee

Date of Statehood: Became the 27th state on March 3, 1845

Largest Cities (by population): Jacksonville, Miami, Tampa, Saint Petersburg, Hialeah, Orlando

Flower: Orange blossom

Tree: Cabbage palmetto

Bird: Mockingbird

State Motto: "In God We Trust"

Economy:
Agriculture – Cattle, citrus, dairy products, nursery stock, sugarcane, vegetables
Industry – Electrical equipment, food processing, machinery, printing and publishing, tourism, transportation equipment

Famous Floridians

Julian "Cannonball" Adderley
jazz musician

Steve Carlton
baseball player

Fay Dunaway
actress

Zora Neale Hurston
author

Frances Langford
pop singer

Osceola
Seminole leader

Janet Reno
U.S. attorney general

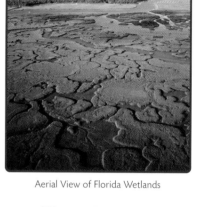

Aerial View of Florida Wetlands

Fun Facts

- The alligator is Florida's official state reptile.

- Miami is the only city in the United States that contains parts of two national parks—Everglades National Park and Biscayne National Park.

- More amusement park visitors come to Orlando than any other city in the United States.

- Lightning strikes Clearwater more often than any other city in the United States.

- U.S. spacecraft are launched from the Kennedy Space Center on Cape Canaveral.

- Many Major League Baseball teams hold spring training in Florida.

GEORGIA The Peach State

Atlanta

England and Spain both made early claims to Georgia. Eventually, British General James Oglethorpe established the first permanent colony in 1733 and held off Spanish invaders in 1742 at the Battle of Bloody Marsh. During the Civil War, Georgia was a Confederate stronghold and the scene of much military action. Union General William T. Sherman burned Atlanta and destroyed a path 60 miles (96 km) wide and 250 miles (402 km) long to the coastline, where he captured Savannah. Georgia is the largest state in the Southeast, and though it is still dominated by agriculture, Atlanta has become a high-tech communications hub for that part of the country.

State Stats

Abbreviation: GA

Area: 59,441 square miles (153,952 km²)

Total Population (2000 Census): 8,186,453

Capital: Atlanta

Date of Statehood: Became the fourth state on January 2, 1788

Largest Cities (by population): Atlanta, Augusta, Columbus, Savannah, Athens, Macon

Flower: Cherokee rose

Tree: Live oak

Bird: Brown thrasher

State Motto: "Wisdom, Justice, and Moderation"

Economy:
Agriculture – Cattle, dairy products, fruits and nuts, hogs, poultry and eggs, vegetables
Industry – Chemical products, electrical equipment, food processing, paper products, textiles and apparel, tourism, transportation equipment

Famous Georgians

James E. "Jimmy" Carter
39th president of the United States

Rebecca Latimer Felton
U.S. senator

Martin Luther King Jr.
civil rights activist

Gladys Knight
pop singer

Jackie Robinson
baseball player

Alice Walker
author

Joanne Woodward
actress

Confederate Memorial at Stone Mountain

Fun Facts

- The bloodiest battle in American history was the Battle of Chickamauga in Georgia during the Civil War.

- In the town of Gainesville, it is against the law to eat chicken with a fork.

- Georgia was named after England's King George II.

- The world's biggest college campus is found at Berry College in Rome. The campus stretches for 28,000 acres (11,300 ha).

- Georgia leads the nation in production of peaches, pecans, and peanuts.

- Coca-Cola was invented in Atlanta. Dr. John S. Pemberton created the popular soft drink in May 1886.

State Flag

Honolulu

Sitting 2,397 miles (3,857 km) west-southwest of San Francisco, Hawaii is a chain of islands that is 1,523 miles (2,451 km) long. Hawaii was settled by Polynesians between AD 300 and 600 and was visited by British sea captain James Cook in 1778. During the 19th century, U.S. business interests became involved with Hawaii, and in 1900, Hawaii became a U.S. territory. Cane sugar and pineapple became the main crops grown there. The Japanese attack on the U.S. Navy base at Pearl Harbor led to the U.S. entry into World War II (1939–45). Today, its desirable weather and beautiful beaches make Hawaii a vacationer's paradise.

State Stats

Abbreviation: HI

Area: 10,932 square miles (28,314 km^2)

Total Population (2000 Census): 1,211,537

Capital: Honolulu

Date of Statehood: Became the 50th state on August 21, 1959

Largest Cities (by population): Honolulu, Hilo, Kailua, Kaneohe, Waipahu, Pearl City

Flower: Hibiscus (Pua aloalo)

Tree: Candlenut

Bird: Nene

State Motto: "The Life of the Land Is Perpetuated in Righteousness"

Economy:
Agriculture – Livestock, macadamia nuts, nursery stock, pineapples, sugarcane
Industry – Apparel, fabricated metal products, food processing, stone, clay, and glass products, tourism

Famous Hawaiians

Tia Carrere
actress

Jean Erdman
dancer, choreographer

Daniel K. Inouye
U.S. senator

Duke Paoa Kahanamoku
Olympic swimmer, surfer

Kamehameha I
first Hawaiian king

Liliuokalani
Hawaiian queen, final monarch of Hawaii

Ellison Onizuka
astronaut

Kauai Beach
Provided by Kauai Visitors Bureau (www.kauaidiscovery.com)

Fun Facts

- The islands of Hawaii were created thousands of years ago when undersea volcanoes erupted.

- Eight main islands make up the state of Hawaii.

- The Hawaiian alphabet consists of just twelve letters. They are A, E, H, I, K, L, M, N, O, P, U, and W.

- Hawaii is far from everywhere! It's 2,390 miles (3,846 km) from California, 4,900 miles (7,884 km) from China, 3,850 miles (6,195 km) from Japan, and 5,280 miles (8,496 km) from the Philippines.

- The only royal palace in the United States is Iolanai Palace on the island of Oahu.

- Of the 50 states, Hawaii is the only one in which coffee is grown.

IDAHO The Gem State

★
Boise

The area that became Idaho was part of the region explored by the Lewis and Clark expedition in the early 1800s. The first permanent U.S. settlement was established by the Mormons, in Franklin, in 1860. When gold was discovered at Orofino Creek that year, many prospectors flooded into the territory, but when the gold rush ended, Idaho was left with little more than ghost towns. The population increased over the next 100 years, and the 1990s saw a boom in both the high-tech industries, centered in Boise, and the winter sports, resort, and tourism industries, which now rank as the most profitable in the state.

State Stats

Abbreviation: ID

Area: 83,574 square miles (216,457 km²)

Total Population (2000 Census): 1,293,953

Capital: Boise

Date of Statehood: Became the 43rd state on July 3, 1890

Largest Cities (by population): Boise, Nampa, Idaho Falls, Pocatello, Meridian, Coeur d'Alene

Flower: Syringa

Tree: Western white pine

Bird: Mountain bluebird

State Motto: "It Is Forever"

Economy:
Agriculture – Barley, cattle, dairy products, potatoes, sugar beets, wheat
Industry – Chemical products, food processing, lumber and wood products, machinery, paper products, silver and other mining, tourism

Famous Idahoans

Carol R. Brink
author

Frank Church
U.S. senator

Harmon Killebrew
baseball player

Ezra Pound
poet

Sacagawea
Shoshone interpreter for Meriwether Lewis and William Clark

Picabo Street
Olympic skier

Lana Turner
actress

Sawtooth Mountain Range

Fun Facts

- Philo T. Farnsworth, the inventor of an early television, grew up in Rigby.

- The Idaho Champion Western Red Cedar Tree, is 177 feet (54 m) tall and has an 18-foot (5.5-m) diameter.

- From Heaven's Gate Lookout, you can see into four different states.

- The tallest sand dune in North America – 470 feet (143 m) high – is located in Bruneau Dunes State Park.

- The world's largest population of nesting eagles, hawks, and falcons is found in the Birds of Prey Wildlife Area.

- It is illegal in Idaho to give someone a box of candy that is over 50 pounds (23 kg).

ILLINOIS The Prairie State

★ Springfield

In 1699, French settlers established the first permanent settlement in Illinois. England got the region after the French and Indian War (1754–63), and the area figured prominently in the Revolutionary War and the wars with Native Americans in the early 19th century. When the Erie Canal opened in 1825, settlers began moving to Illinois in greater numbers. Illinois is home to the classic American story of Abraham Lincoln, who started out working as a farm laborer and became one of the greatest presidents in U.S. history. The great city of Chicago is known for its museums and architecture.

State Stats

Abbreviation: IL

Area: 57,918 square miles (150,008 km²)

Total Population (2000 Census): 12,419,293

Capital: Springfield

Date of Statehood: Became the 21st state on December 3, 1818

Largest Cities (by population): Chicago, Aurora, Rockford, Naperville, Joliet, Springfield

Flower: Purple violet

Tree: White oak

Bird: Cardinal

State Motto: "State Sovereignty, National Union"

Economy:
Agriculture – Cattle, corn, dairy products, hogs, soybeans, wheat
Industry – Chemical products, coal, electrical equipment, fabricated metal products, food processing, machinery, petroleum, printing and publishing, transportation equipment

Famous Illinoisans

Jane Addams
social reformer

Gillian Anderson
actress

Jack Benny
comedian

Walt Disney
animator, studio head

Betty Friedan
author, women's rights activist

Dorothy Hamill
ice skater

Ronald Reagan
40th president of the United States

Chicago's Buckingham Fountain

Fun Facts

- The ice cream sundae was invented in Evanston.

- The largest public library in the world is located in Chicago. The Chicago Public Library has more than two million books.

- The first skyscraper ever built was constructed in 1885 in Chicago.

- The Nabisco factory is in Chicago. It produces 16 billion Oreo cookies every year.

- In 1865, Illinois became the first state to vote in favor of ending slavery when it ratified the 13th Amendment to the Constitution.

- It is illegal for boys (but not for girls) to throw snowballs at trees in the town of Mount Pulaski.

INDIANA The Hoosier State

Indianapolis

Indiana was part of the region in which the French and British struggled for control during the 17th century. The British finally gained dominance in 1763, following the French and Indian War. Indiana was also the scene of major battles during the Revolutionary War. In the 19th century, Indiana was the site of several experimental communities, including one at New Harmony, where a communal colony gained distinction as a noted cultural and scientific center. Today, Indiana's Lake Michigan waterfront — which is 41 miles (66 km) long — is one of the world's leading industrial centers.

State Stats

Abbreviation: IN

Area: 36,420 square miles (94,328 km²)

Total Population (2000 Census): 6,080,485

Capital: Indianapolis

Date of Statehood: Became the 19th state on December 11, 1816

Largest Cities (by population): Indianapolis, Fort Wayne, Evansville, South Bend, Gary, Hammond

Flower: Peony

Tree: Yellow poplar

Bird: Cardinal

State Motto: "The Crossroads of America"

Economy:
Agriculture – Cattle, corn, dairy products, eggs, hogs, soybeans
Industry – Chemical products, electrical equipment, machinery, petroleum and coal products, steel, transportation equipment

Famous Indianans

Anne Baxter
actress

Virgil Grissom
astronaut

David Letterman
comedian, television host

Red Skelton
comedian

Twyla Tharp
dancer, choreographer

Jessamyn West
author

Wilbur Wright
inventor

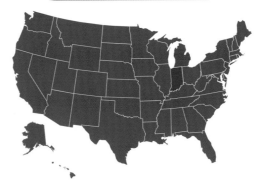

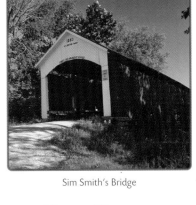

Sim Smith's Bridge

Fun Facts

- On May 4, 1871, in the town of Fort Wayne, the first professional baseball game took place.

- Indiana is home to more than 100 species of native trees.

- Each Christmas, the town of Santa Claus, Indiana, gets more than half a million letters— for obvious reasons!

- Of the 50 states, Indiana contains the most miles of interstate highway per square mile.

- Much of the limestone quarried for construction in the United States comes from Indiana.

- Explorers Meriwether Lewis and William Clark began their expedition through the vast Northwest Territory from Fort Vincennes.

IOWA
The Hawkeye State

State Flag

★ Des Moines

Iowa was named after the Sioux tribe *Ayuhwa*. This name means "beautiful land" or "sleepy ones." The state nickname, the Hawkeye State, is in honor of Chief Black Hawk, a Sauk and Fox leader. In 1788, Julien Dubuque, Iowa's first white settler, started to mine lead near Dubuque. In 1803, the Iowa area was bought from France by the United States as part of the Louisiana Purchase. In the 1930s, an unknown artist named Grant Wood painted *American Gothic*. The famous painting showed an Iowan farmer and his daughter looking very serious. Today, most of Iowa remains farmland—a whopping 97 percent!

State Stats

Abbreviation: IA

Area: 56,276 square miles (145,755 km²)

Total Population (2000 Census): 2,926,324

Capital: Des Moines

Date of Statehood: Became the 29th state on December 28, 1846

Largest Cities (by population): Des Moines, Cedar Rapids, Davenport, Sioux City, Waterloo, Iowa City

Flower: Wild rose

Tree: Oak

Bird: Eastern goldfinch

State Motto: "Our Liberties We Prize and Our Rights We Will Maintain"

Economy:
Agriculture – Corn, dairy products, eggs, grain, hay, oats, popcorn, soybeans
Industry – Farm machinery, fertilizer and other agricultural chemicals, food processing, meatpacking, motor vehicle parts, pesticides

Famous Iowans

Bess Streeter Aldrich
author

John Vincent Atanasoff and Clifford Berry
inventors of the digital computer

William F. "Buffalo Bill" Cody
Wild West showman

Lee DeForest
inventor

Mamie Doud Eisenhower
first lady

Herbert Hoover
31st president of the United States

Lillian Russell
opera singer

Iowa Cornfield

Fun Facts

- Cedar Rapids has one of the largest cereal mills in the United States.

- The Effigy Mounds at Marquette are earthen mounds built by prehistoric Native Americans. The mounds are shaped like animals.

- Indianola is home to the National Balloon Museum.

- In the United States, Iowa ranks first in soybean, egg, corn, and hog production.

- The largest strawberry in the world can be found in Strawberry Point. It is a giant model of a strawberry that sits atop a sign announcing the town's name.

- Of all state names, "Iowa" is the only one that begins with two vowels.

KANSAS The Sunflower State

State Flag

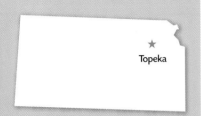

★ Topeka

Although Spanish explorers were the first Europeans to travel in Kansas, the French made early claims to the region. The territory went back and forth between France and Spain until it was finally sold to the United States in 1803 as part of the Louisiana Purchase. Meriwether Lewis and William Clark explored the region in the early 1800s, and the first European settlements were established in 1827. During the Civil War, much bloody conflict took place in Kansas between pro- and anti-slavery forces. Today, the state is known for its wheat fields, cattle ranches, and oil wells.

State Stats

Abbreviation: KS

Area: 82,282 square miles (213,110 km²)

Total Population (2000 Census): 2,688,418

Capital: Topeka

Date of Statehood: Became the 34th state on January 29, 1861

Largest Cities (by population): Wichita, Overland Park, Kansas City, Topeka, Olathe, Lawrence

Flower: Sunflower

Tree: Cottonwood

Bird: Western meadowlark

State Motto: "To the Stars Through Difficulties"

Economy:
Agriculture – Cattle, corn, hogs, sorghum, soybeans, wheat
Industry – Apparel, chemical products, food processing, machinery, mining, petroleum, printing and publishing, transportation equipment

Famous Kansans

Gwendolyn Brooks
poet

Walter P. Chrysler
auto manufacturer

Amelia Earhart
aviator

Walter Johnson
baseball player

Buster Keaton
actor

Gordon Parks
film director, writer, photographer

Vivian Vance
actress

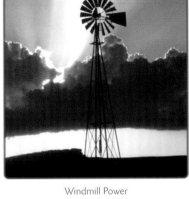

Windmill Power

Fun Facts

- Hutchinson has an enormous grain elevator that is 0.5 miles (0.8 km) long.

- An old law in Kansas made it illegal to serve ice cream on cherry pie. That law is no longer on the books.

- Susan Madora Salter was elected to office in Argonia in 1887, becoming the first female mayor of a city in the United States.

- Dodge City has the blustery distinction of being the windiest city in the nation.

- Kansan Hattie McDaniel was the first African-American woman to win an Academy Award, for her role in the 1939 film *Gone with the Wind*.

- Kansas produced enough wheat for 33 billion loaves of bread in 1990.

17

State Flag

★
Frankfort

Kentucky was the first region west of the Allegheny Mountains to be settled by Europeans. The first colony was established in 1774. Originally, Kentucky was part of Virginia, but it gained statehood in 1792. As a slaveholding state with a large abolitionist population, Kentucky was caught in conflict during the Civil War, supplying soldiers to both the Union and Confederate armies. Today, the state is known for producing tobacco and whiskey and for raising horses. Each year, the world-famous horse race, the Kentucky Derby, is held at Churchill Downs in Louisville.

State Stats

Abbreviation: KY

Area: 40,411 square miles (104,664 km²)

Total Population (2000 Census): 4,041,769

Capital: Frankfort

Date of Statehood: Became the 15th state on June 1, 1792

Largest Cities (by population): Lexington-Fayette, Louisville, Owensboro, Bowling Green, Covington, Richmond

Flower: Goldenrod

Tree: Tulip poplar

Bird: Cardinal

State Motto: "United We Stand, Divided We Fall"

Economy:
Agriculture – Cattle, corn, dairy products, hogs, horses, soybeans, tobacco
Industry – Chemical products, coal, electrical equipment, food processing, machinery, tobacco products, tourism, transportation equipment

Famous Kentuckians

Muhammad Ali
boxer

Rosemary Clooney
pop singer

Jefferson Davis
president of the Confederacy

Irene Dunne
actress

Abraham Lincoln
16th president of the United States

Loretta Lynn
country singer

Diane Sawyer
broadcast journalist

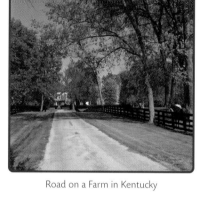

Road on a Farm in Kentucky

Fun Facts

- The first Kentucky Fried Chicken restaurant was opened in the town of Corbin in 1952.

- The longest cave in the world is Mammoth Cave in south-central Kentucky.

- The Kentucky Derby, held each year in May, is the oldest horse race in the country.

- More than $6 billion is kept at Fort Knox in underground vaults.

- Jefferson Davis, president of the Confederacy, and Abraham Lincoln, president of the Union, were born less than 100 miles (161 km) from each other in Kentucky.

- In 1893, two sisters from Louisville – Mildred J. Hill and Patty Smith Hill – wrote the song "Happy Birthday to You."

LOUISIANA The Pelican State

★
Baton Rouge

Spanish explorers were in Louisiana as early as 1519, but René-Robert Cavelier, Sieur de la Salle, claimed the region for King Louis XIV of France in 1682, naming the area after the king. Spain took control of Louisiana in 1763, but it returned to French hands in 1800. Three years later, Napoleon Bonaparte sold it to the United States as part of the Louisiana Purchase. After the Civil War, Louisiana's economy suffered greatly, but it began to recover in the early 20th century with the discovery of oil and natural gas in the state. In 2005, Hurricane Katrina devastated the Louisiana coastline and flooded the city of New Orleans.

State Stats

Abbreviation: LA

Area: 51,843 square miles (134,273 km²)

Total Population (2000 Census): 4,468,976

Capital: Baton Rouge

Date of Statehood: Became the 18th state on April 30, 1812

Largest Cities (by population): New Orleans, Baton Rouge, Shreveport, Lafayette, Lake Charles, Kenner

Flower: Magnolia

Tree: Bald cypress

Bird: Eastern brown pelican

State Motto: "Union, Justice, and Confidence"

Economy:
Agriculture – Cattle, cotton, dairy products, poultry and eggs, rice, seafood, soybeans, sugarcane
Industry – Chemical products, food processing, paper products, petroleum and coal products, tourism, transportation equipment

Famous Louisianans

Louis Armstrong
jazz musician

Terry Bradshaw
football player

Truman Capote
author

Lillian Hellman
playwright

Mahalia Jackson
gospel singer

Huey P. Long
governor of Louisiana

Cokie Roberts
journalist

French Quarter in New Orleans

Fun Facts

- The tallest state capitol building anywhere in the United States can be found in Louisiana. It stands 450 feet (137 m) tall.

- Louisiana is the only state in America that does not use the term *county* to describe its sections. They are called "parishes" instead.

- In 1862, the Confederate Louisiana Native Guards became the first U.S. army in which African-Americans could become officers.

- A town called Jean Lafitte was once used as a hideout for pirates.

- The town of Mamou is known as "the Cajun Music Capital of the World."

- To honor Native Americans, the city flag of Baton Rouge has a field of crimson on it.

The Pine Tree State

Augusta ★

Although British explorer John Cabot visited the Maine coast as early as 1498, the first British colony was not set up until 1623. When the Revolutionary War began in 1775, the very first naval battle between the colonists and the British was fought off Machias on the Maine coast. After being part of the Massachusetts government for many years, Maine finally became a separate state as part of the Missouri Compromise in 1820. Today, Maine is one of the nation's biggest producers of blueberries, pulp-paper, and lobsters. Its beautiful shoreline, lakes, and mountains also make Maine a popular tourist destination.

State Stats

Abbreviation: ME

Area: 35,387 square miles (91,652 km²)

Total Population (2000 Census): 1,274,923

Capital: Augusta

Date of Statehood: Became the 23rd state on March 15, 1820

Largest Cities (by population): Portland, Lewiston, Bangor, South Portland, Auburn, Biddeford

Flowers: White pinecone and tassel

Tree: Eastern white pine

Bird: Chickadee

State Motto: "I Lead"

Economy:
Agriculture – Apples, blueberries, cattle, dairy products, potatoes, poultry and eggs, seafood
Industry – Electrical equipment, food processing, leather products, lumber and wood products, paper products, textiles, tourism

Famous Mainers

Dorothea Dix
nurse, social activist

John Ford
film director

Stephen King
author

Linda Lavin
actress

Henry Wadsworth Longfellow
poet

Joan Benoit Samuelson
marathon runner

Margaret Chase Smith
U.S. senator

Wood Island Lighthouse

Fun Facts

- Maine is the only state that shares a border with just one other state.

- About 90 percent of all lobsters caught in the United States come from Maine.

- The first incorporated city in the United States was York in 1642.

- Ninety-nine percent of the blueberries harvested in the United States come from Maine.

- Maine is the only state with a one-syllable name.

- Maine's Senator Margaret Chase Smith was the first woman to run for president of the United States, in 1964.

MARYLAND The Old Line State

Annapolis ★

In 1608, Captain John Smith explored Chesapeake Bay. In 1632, Lord Baltimore settled an English colony there. From 1763 to 1767, Charles Mason and Jeremiah Dixon surveyed Maryland's border with Pennsylvania. The line they surveyed, which eventually extended more than 200 miles (322 km) west, became known as the Mason-Dixon line. During the Civil War, Maryland was a slave state but remained in the Union, so some members of the same families fought on opposite sides. Maryland's Eastern Shore along Chesapeake Bay is one of the nation's longest waterfronts, and the bay is famous for its crabs.

State Stats

Abbreviation: MD

Area: 12,407 square miles (32,134 km²)

Total Population (2000 Census): 5,296,486

Capital: Annapolis

Date of Statehood: Became the seventh state on April 28, 1788

Largest Cities (by population): Baltimore, Gaithersburg, Frederick, Rockville, Bowie, Hagerstown

Flower: Black-eyed Susan

Tree: White oak

Bird: Baltimore oriole

State Motto: "Strong Deeds, Gentle Words"

Economy:
Agriculture – Cattle, corn, dairy products, nursery stock, poultry and eggs, seafood, soybeans
Industry – Chemical products, coal, electrical equipment, food processing, machinery, printing and publishing, tourism, transportation equipment

Famous Marylanders

Florence Riefle Bahr
artist

Philip Glass
composer

Billie Holiday
jazz singer

Thurgood Marshall
U.S. Supreme Court justice

H. L. Mencken
writer

George Herman "Babe" Ruth
baseball player

Harriet Tubman
abolitionist

Camden Yards

Fun Facts

- Baltimore is the site of the National Aquarium.

- The first successful manned balloon launch in the United States took place in Baltimore on June 24, 1784.

- In 1814, the British bombardment of Fort McHenry inspired Francis Scott Key to write the words to "The Star Spangled Banner."

- In 1844, Samuel F. B. Morse received the first telegraph message ever sent in Bladensburg.

- The U.S. Naval Academy was established in Annapolis in 1845.

- Some of the land that used to be part of Maryland was given up by the state in order to create Washington, D. C., the nation's capital.

State Flag

Boston ★

Pilgrims seeking religious freedom settled Massachusetts in 1620. Massachusetts was one the most important of the Thirteen Colonies in organizing resistance to British oppression. In 1773, the Boston Tea Party protested unfair taxation. Minutemen soldiers from Massachusetts started the Revolutionary War by battling British troops at Lexington and Concord in 1775. After the war, Massachusetts became a leader in education, the arts, and industry. Today, tourism, based on both its rich history and its beautiful beaches like those at Cape Cod, is a main part of the Massachusetts economy.

State Stats

Abbreviation: MA

Area: 10,555 square miles (27,337 km²)

Total Population (2000 Census): 6,349,097

Capital: Boston

Date of Statehood: Became the sixth state on February 6, 1788

Largest Cities (by population): Boston, Worcester, Springfield, Lowell, Cambridge, Brockton

Flower: Mayflower

Tree: American elm

Bird: Chickadee

State Motto: "By the Sword We Seek Peace, but Peace Only Under Liberty"

Economy:
Agriculture – Cranberries, dairy products, nursery stock, seafood, vegetables
Industry – Electrical equipment, machinery, printing and publishing, scientific instruments, tourism

Famous Massachusettians

Susan B. Anthony
women's rights activist

Clara Barton
founder of the American Red Cross

Rachel Fuller Brown
inventor

Emily Dickinson
poet

Benjamin Franklin
statesman, scientist

John F. Kennedy
35th president of the United States

Edgar Allan Poe
author

Rockport

Fun Facts

- In 1897, the first subway system ever built in the United States was constructed in Boston.

- Four U.S. presidents were born in Norfolk County: John Adams, John Quincy Adams, John F. Kennedy, and George H. W. Bush.

- The only visible portion of Plymouth Rock, which only covers just a few square feet, has the date 1620 cut into its surface.

- The first game of basketball ever played was in Springfield in 1891.

- The first public elementary school in the United States was founded in Dorchester in 1639.

- Plymouth was the site of the very first Thanksgiving Day celebration in 1621.

State Flag

Lansing ★

French explorers began arriving in Michigan in the early 1600s, and the first permanent European colony was established in 1688. England obtained the territory from France following the French and Indian War. After the Revolutionary War, Michigan became part of the United States. Michigan borders on four of the five Great Lakes and is divided into Upper and Lower Peninsulas by the Straits of Mackinac, which link Lakes Michigan and Huron. These two parts of the state are connected by the Mackinac Bridge, one of the world's longest suspension bridges. Michigan is well known for its production of automobiles.

State Stats

Abbreviation: MI

Area: 96,810 square miles (250,738 km²)

Total Population (2000 Census): 9,938,444

Capital: Lansing

Date of Statehood: Became the 26th state on January 26, 1837

Largest Cities (by population): Detroit, Grand Rapids, Warren, Sterling Heights, Flint, Lansing

Flower: Apple blossom

Tree: Eastern white pine

Bird: Robin

State Motto: "If You Seek a Pleasant Peninsula, Look About You."

Economy:
Agriculture – Apples, blueberries, cattle, corn, dairy products, hogs, nursery stock, soybeans, vegetables
Industry – Chemical products, fabricated metal products, food processing, machinery, mining, motor vehicles and parts, tourism

Famous Michiganders

Edna Ferber
author

Henry Ford
industrialist

Julie Krone
jockey

Charles A. Lindbergh
aviator

Madonna
singer, actress

Lily Tomlin
actress

Stevie Wonder
rock and soul musician, songwriter

Lake Michigan

Fun Facts

- The Mackinac Bridge crosses 5 miles (8 km) over the Straits of Mackinac.

- Vernors Ginger Ale became the nation's first soda pop made in Detroit in 1866.

- The Detroit Zoo was the first U.S. zoo to use naturalistic, open-air environments.

- The first regularly scheduled airline passenger service in the United States started in 1926 between Grand Rapids and Detroit.

- Because of the Great Lakes, Michigan has more miles of shore than any other state except Alaska.

- Detroit's nickname is "the Motor City" because of all the cars that have been produced there.

MINNESOTA The North Star State

St. Paul ★

French explorers, missionaries, and fur traders were the first Europeans to visit Minnesota, which was claimed for Louis XIV of France by Daniel Greysolon, Sieur Duluth, in 1679. The United States acquired the eastern part of the state from England after the Revolutionary War and the western portion from France as part of the Louisiana Purchase in 1803. Minnesota is a state rich in natural resources and agriculture. Known for its ten thousand lakes, Minnesota is a popular tourist destination, especially among fans of winter sports and the culture of the twin cities of Minneapolis and St. Paul.

State Stats

Abbreviation: MN

Area: 86,943 square miles (225,182 km²)

Total Population (2000 Census): 4,919,479

Capital: St. Paul

Date of Statehood: Became the 32nd state on May 11, 1858

Largest Cities (by population): Minneapolis, Saint Paul, Rochester, Duluth, Bloomington, Plymouth

Flower: Pink and white lady's slipper

Tree: Red pine

Bird: Common loon

State Motto: "The Star of the North"

Economy:
Agriculture – Cattle, corn, dairy products, hogs, soybeans, turkeys, wheat
Industry – Electrical equipment, fabricated metal products, food processing, machinery, mining, printing and publishing, tourism

Famous Minnesotans

Bob Dylan
folk and rock musician, songwriter

F. Scott Fitzgerald
author

Judy Garland
singer, actress

Jean Paul Getty
oil executive

Kate Millett
women's rights activist

Jane Russell
actress

Charles M. Schulz
cartoonist

Aerial View of Minneapolis Skyline

Fun Facts

- Bloomington's Mall of America is huge – You could fit 78 football fields inside!

- The Old Log Theater in Minneapolis is the oldest continuously operating theater in the United States.

- Minnesota has more miles of shoreline than Florida, California, and Hawaii put together.

- Only one U.S. arena has hosted a World Series, a Super Bowl, and an NCAA basketball championship – the Metrodome.

- The Minneapolis Public Library was the first library to create a children's department in 1889.

- The Milky Way candy bar was first created by Frank C. Mars of Minnesota.

MISSISSIPPI The Magnolia State

France and England each had colonies in Mississippi during the 1600s, and the United States acquired the territory in 1783. For more than 100 years, cotton was the backbone of the Mississippi economy, although in the 20th century, the state's farmers began to grow other crops, such as corn, peanuts, and rice.

State Stats

Abbreviation: MS

Area: 48,434 square miles (125,444 km²)

Total Population (2000 Census): 2,844,658

Capital: Jackson

Date of Statehood: Became the 20th state on December 10, 1817

Largest Cities (by population): Jackson, Gulfport, Biloxi, Hattiesburg, Meridian, Greenville

Flower: Magnolia

Tree: Southern magnolia

Bird: Mockingbird

State Motto: "By Valor and Arms"

Economy:
Agriculture – Catfish, cattle, cotton, dairy products, poultry, rice, soybeans
Industry – Apparel, electrical machinery, food processing, furniture, lumber and wood products, transportation equipment

State Flag

Jackson

Fun Facts

- The Old Spanish Fort Museum in Pascagoula has as one of its exhibits the world's largest shrimp.

- Edward Adolf Barq Sr. invented root beer in 1898 in the town of Biloxi and started the company that still bears his name.

MISSOURI The Show Me State

French fur traders set up the first permanent Missouri settlement in 1735, and the city of St. Louis was established in 1764. The United States got the territory as part of the Louisiana Purchase in 1803. Missouri is known as "the Gateway to the West." The easternmost point of the Pony Express route started there.

State Stats

Abbreviation: MO

Area: 69,709 square miles

Total Population (2000 Census): 5,595,211

Capital: Jefferson City

Date of Statehood: Became the 24th state on August 10, 1821

Largest Cities (by population): Kansas City, Saint Louis, Springfield, Independence, Columbia, Lee's Summit

Flower: Hawthorn

Tree: Flowering dogwood

Bird: Bluebird

State Motto: "The Welfare of the People Shall Be the Supreme Law"

Economy:
Agriculture – Cattle, corn, dairy products, hogs, poultry and eggs, soybeans
Industry – Chemical products, electrical equipment, fabricated metal products, food processing, transportation equipment

State Flag

Jefferson City

Fun Facts

- Captain Albert Berry was the first person to successfully parachute jump from an airplane. He took his historic leap in St. Louis in 1912.

- Richard Blechyden invented iced tea in 1904 at the St. Louis World's Fair by adding ice to a cup of tea.

MONTANA The Treasure State

★
Helena

The area that is now Montana was first explored by the French in the 1740s and was acquired by the United States in 1803 as part of the Louisiana Purchase. By 1846, American forts and trading posts had been established throughout the territory. The Battle of the Little Big Horn, also known as Custer's Last Stand, took place in the southeast part of the state in 1876. In this famous battle, Cheyenne and Sioux warriors defeated General George Armstrong Custer and more than 200 of his men. Mining played a huge role in the state's early growth. Today, fields of grain cover much of the state's plains.

State Stats

Abbreviation: MT

Area: 147,046 square miles

Total Population (2000 Census): 902,195

Capital: Helena

Date of Statehood: Became the 41st state on November 8,1889

Largest Cities (by population): Billings, Missoula, Great Falls, Butte–Silver Bow, Bozeman, Helena

Flower: Bitterroot

Tree: Ponderosa pine

Bird: Western meadowlark

State Motto: "Gold and Silver"

Economy:
Agriculture – Barley, cattle, hay, hogs, sugar beets, wheat
Industry – Food processing, lumber and wood products, mining, tourism

Famous Montanans

Dorothy Baker
author

Gary Cooper
actor

Chet Huntley
television newscaster

Evel Knievel
daredevil

Myrna Loy
actress

David Lynch
filmmaker

Jeanette Rankin
first woman elected to Congress

Glacier National Park

Fun Facts

- There were more millionaires per capita in Helena in 1888 than in any other city in the world.

- The first national park in the United States was Yellowstone National Park, which is partly in southern Montana and partly in Wyoming.

- More grizzly bears live in Montana than in any other state except Alaska.

- There are more elk in Montana than in any other state in the United States.

- Close to 10,000 pelicans migrate to Montana's Medicine Lake each spring.

- Water from the rivers of Montana ends up in three different oceans.

Lincoln
★

French fur traders first visited Nebraska in the late 1600s. After the United States acquired the region as part of the Louisiana Purchase in 1803, Meriwether Lewis and William Clark explored the territory during their expedition from 1804 to 1806. The first permanent European settlement was established at Bellevue in 1823. In 1865, the Union Pacific began building its transcontinental railroad at Omaha. Oil was discovered in Nebraska in 1939, and natural gas was found in 1949. Today, Nebraska is one of the nation's leading producers of wheat and corn.

State Stats

Abbreviation: NE

Area: 77,358 square miles

Total Population (2000 Census): 1,711,263

Capital: Lincoln

Date of Statehood: Became the 37th state on March 1, 1867

Largest Cities (by population): Omaha, Lincoln, Bellevue, Grand Island, Kearney, Fremont

Flower: Goldenrod

Tree: Cottonwood

Bird: Western meadowlark

State Motto: "Equality Before the Law"

Economy:
Agriculture – Cattle, corn, hogs, sorghum, soybeans, wheat
Industry – Electrical equipment, food processing, machinery, printing and publishing

Famous Nebraskans

Grace Abbott
social reformer

Marlon Brando
actor

Gerald R. Ford
38th president of the United States

Susette La Flesche
artist

Malcolm X
civil rights activist

Red Cloud
Sioux chief

Mari Sandoz
author

Eagle Rock

Fun Facts

- If you add up the total miles of all Nebraska rivers, no state has more.

- Arbor Day was created in 1872 in Nebraska by J. Sterling Morton.

- The town of Kearney sits precisely at the midpoint of the United States, between Boston and San Francisco.

- A law in Blue Hill states that no woman wearing a "hat that would scare a timid person" is allowed to eat onions in public.

- The first time in U.S. history that two women faced off in an election for governor was in Nebraska in 1986.

- On July 4, 1882, Buffalo Bill Cody ran his first rodeo, in North Platte.

NEVADA   The Silver State

★ Carson City

Trappers and traders first entered Nevada in the 1820s. In the 1840s, Kit Carson explored the Great Basin and Sierra Nevada regions. The United States acquired Nevada in 1848, after the Mexican-American War. Nevada was suddenly made famous in 1859 with the discovery of the Comstock Lode, the richest silver deposit ever found in the United States. The Comstock mines there have produced large quantities of silver, gold, zinc, copper, lead, and mercury. In 1931, Nevada introduced gambling, which attracted visitors to casinos in Las Vegas and Reno and remains the state's main draw for tourists.

State Stats

Abbreviation: NV

Area: 110,567 square miles (286,368 km²)

Total Population (2000 Census): 1,998,257

Capital: Carson City

Date of Statehood: Became the 36th state on October 31, 1864

Largest Cities (by population): Las Vegas, Henderson, Reno, North Las Vegas, Sparks, Carson City

Flower: Sagebrush

Tree: Bristlecone pine

Bird: Mountain bluebird

State Motto: "All for Our Country"

Economy:
Agriculture – Cattle, dairy products, hay, potatoes
Industry – Electrical equipment, food processing, machinery, mining, printing and publishing, tourism

Famous Nevadans

Eva Adams
director of the U.S. Mint

Andre Agassi
tennis player

Ben Alexander
actor

Helen Delich Bentley
journalist

Thelma "Pat" Nixon
first lady

Harry M. Reid
U.S. senator

Sarah Hopkins Winnemucca
author, Paiute interpreter, peacemaker

Las Vegas Street Scene

Fun Facts

- Nevada's average rainfall is only 7 inches (17.8 cm) per year.

- Most of Nevada is uninhabited, sagebrush-covered desert.

- In the entire world, only South Africa produces more gold than Nevada.

- In 1931, Nevada introduced liberal divorce laws. Couples seeking easy divorces flocked to Reno and Las Vegas, which became known as "the Divorce Capitals of the World."

- The kangaroo rat, a native of Nevada, can go through its whole life without drinking water.

- In 1960, Nevada had 16,067 slot machines. By 1999, the number had grown to 205,726!

NEW HAMPSHIRE The Granite State

Concord
★

British settlers first arrived in New Hampshire in 1623 to establish a fishing colony near present-day Dover. In 1630, Captain John Mason founded Portsmouth. New Hampshire was part of Massachusetts until 1679, when it became a separate British colony. New Hampshire delegates were the first to sign the Declaration of Independence on July 4, 1776, and the state played an important role during the Revolutionary War. Thanks to the great amount of waterpower from its rivers, New Hampshire has always thrived as a manufacturing state. It also attract many visitors to its beautiful landscapes, scenic lakes, and the majestic White Mountains.

State Stats

Abbreviation: NH

Area: 9,351 square miles (24,219 km²)

Total Population (2000 Census): 1,235,786

Capital: Concord

Date of Statehood: Became the ninth state on June 21, 1788

Largest Cities (by population): Manchester, Nashua, Concord, Derry, Rochester, Salem

Flower: Purple lilac

Tree: Paper birch

Bird: Purple finch

State Motto: "Live Free or Die"

Economy:
Agriculture – Apples, cattle, dairy products, eggs, nursery stock
Industry – Electrical equipment, machinery, rubber and plastic products, tourism

Famous New Hampshirites

Amy Beach
composer

Sarah Josepha Hale
editor

John Irving
author

Franklin Pierce
14th president of the United States

Alan Shepard
astronaut

Celia Laighton Thaxter
poet

Daniel Webster
statesman

Autumn in New Hampshire

Fun Facts

- New Hampshire was the first of the Thirteen Colonies to break away from England.

- The nation's first free public library opened in Peterborough in 1833.

- The first potato planted in the United States was sown in Londonderry Common Field in 1719.

- About 400 women who worked at the Dover Cotton Factory walked out on December 30, 1828, beginning the first women's strike in the country.

- Alan Shepard, from East Derry, was the first American to go into space.

- New Hampshire is one of the top producers of maple syrup in the nation.

NEW JERSEY The Garden State

Trenton ★

New Jersey began as part of the Dutch colony of New York. After the Dutch lost New York to the British in 1664, New Jersey became a separate English colony, but it did not get its own governor until 1738. Because of its location between the key cities of New York and Philadelphia, New Jersey was an important strategic location during the Revolutionary War. Today, chemical production is the number-one industry, although 20 percent of the state is covered by farmland. The Jersey shore, a beautiful stretch of ocean beaches — including Atlantic City, where gambling is legal — attracts many tourists.

State Stats

Abbreviation: NJ

Area: 8,722 square miles (22,590 km²)

Total Population (2000 Census): 8,414,350

Capital: Trenton

Date of Statehood: Became the third state on December 18, 1787

Largest Cities (by population): Newark, Jersey City, Paterson, Elizabeth, Woodbridge, Edison

Flower: Violet

Tree: Northern red oak

Bird: Eastern goldfinch

State Motto: "Liberty and Prosperity"

Economy:
Agriculture – Dairy products, fruits and nuts, horses, nursery stock, seafood, vegetables
Industry – Chemical products, electrical equipment, food processing, printing and publishing, tourism

Famous New Jerseyites

Bud Abbott and Lou Costello
comedians

Judy Blume
author

Helen Gahagan Douglas
U.S. congresswoman

Allen Ginsberg
poet

Frank Sinatra
pop singer, actor

Ruth St. Denis
dancer, choreographer

Meryl Streep
actress

Atlantic City Beach

Fun Facts

- In New Jersey, an average of 1,030 people live within each square mile (2.6 km²).

- The largest seaport in the United States is in Elizabeth.

- Newark has more auto thefts than New York and Los Angeles combined.

- New Jersey has more diners than any other state.

- One area in New Jersey has seven major shopping malls within a 25-square-mile (65-km²) radius — the largest number of malls in this small an area anywhere on Earth!

- Working in his laboratory in Menlo Park, Thomas Edison created the light bulb, the phonograph, and the movie projector.

NEW MEXICO The Land of Enchantment

Santa Fe

In 1540, Spanish explorer Francisco Vásquez de Coronado, became the first European to enter New Mexico. In 1598, the first Spanish settlement was established on the Rio Grande. Then in 1610, Santa Fe was founded. The United States acquired most of New Mexico as a result of the Mexican-American War. Conflicts with Native Americans continued until 1886, when the great Apache chief Geronimo surrendered to U.S. forces. Starting in 1945, nuclear, solar, and geothermal research has continued at the laboratories in Los Alamos. The world-famous Carlsbad Caverns are a major tourist attraction.

State Stats

Abbreviation: NM

Area: 121,593 square miles (314,926 km²)

Total Population (2000 Census): 1,819,046

Capital: Santa Fe

Date of Statehood: Became the 47th state on January 6, 1912

Largest Cities (by population): Albuquerque, Las Cruces, Santa Fe, Rio Rancho, Roswell, Farmington

Flower: Yucca flower

Tree: Piñon pine

Bird: Roadrunner

State Motto: "It Grows as It Goes"

Economy:
Agriculture – Cattle, chili peppers, dairy products, hay, nursery stock
Industry – Electrical equipment, food processing, petroleum and coal products, printing and publishing, stone, clay, and glass products, tourism

Famous New Mexicans

William Hanna
animator

Ralph Kiner
baseball player, sportscaster

Demi Moore
actress

Kim Stanley
actress

Al and Bobby Unser
auto racers

Victorio
Apache chief

Linda Wertheimer
journalist

Taos Pueblos

Fun Facts

- Sitting at 7,000 feet (2,134 m) above sea level, Santa Fe is the nation's highest capital city.

- At a single point, New Mexico's border meets Arizona, Colorado, and Utah.

- The Anasazi, an ancient native people, lived in New Mexico for 1,300 years. More than 25,000 Anasazi sites have been found in the state.

- On July 16, 1945, the first atomic bomb ever to explode on Earth was set off in a test at a range near Alamogordo.

- The Navajo reservation in New Mexico covers 14 million acres (5.7 million ha).

- Each year in October, the Whole Enchilada Fiesta is held in Las Cruces.

NEW YORK The Empire State

State Flag

Albany ★

New York State's first name was New Netherland when it was settled by the Dutch in 1624. Then the English claimed the land and changed its name to New York to honor the Duke of York. In 1783, George Washington believed New York would become the center of a new empire, and the state's nickname is indeed "the Empire State." New York leads the United States in book publishing. Three-fourths of all books published in the country are published there. The state is second only to California in production of manufactured goods — $80 billion worth of stuff!

State Stats

Abbreviation: NY

Area: 49,576 square miles (128,402 km²)

Total Population (2000 Census): 18,976,457

Capital: Albany

Date of Statehood: Became the 11th state on July 26, 1788

Largest Cities (by population): New York City, Buffalo, Rochester, Yonkers, Syracuse, Albany

Flower: Rose

Tree: Sugar maple

Bird: Bluebird

State Motto: "Excelsior" ("Ever Upward")

Economy:
Agriculture – Apples, cattle, dairy products, nursery stock, vegetables
Industry – Chemical products, electrical equipment, machinery, printing and publishing, scientific instruments, tourism

Famous New Yorkers

Lucille Ball
actress

Maria Callas
opera singer

Lou Gehrig
baseball player

Franklin D. Roosevelt
32nd president of the United States

Margaret Sanger
nurse, women's health advocate

Maurice Sendak
children's book author and illustrator

Edith Wharton
author

Niagara Falls

Fun Facts

- Approximately one-third of the Revolutionary War battles were fought on New York soil.

- One of New York's state parks, the Adirondack Park, is huge — bigger than Grand Canyon, Yosemite, Yellowstone, Olympic, and Glacier National Parks put together!

- The Uncle Sam symbol for the United States originated in Troy.

- The longest toll superhighway in the United States is the Governor Thomas E. Dewey Thruway. It is 641 miles (1,031 km) in length.

- The first state to require automobiles to carry license plates was New York.

- The New York State canal system is 524 miles (843 km) long and has 57 locks.

State Flag

Raleigh ★

English colonists unsuccessfully tried to colonize Roanoke Island in 1585. The first permanent settlements in North Carolina were established by colonists from Virginia in 1653. A decade later, North Carolina became an English colony. Despite much antislavery sentiment within the state, North Carolina joined the Confederacy during the Civil War. Today, North Carolina is the nation's largest producer of furniture, tobacco, bricks, and textiles. Popular tourist attractions include the Blue Ridge and Great Smoky Mountains and the Wright Brothers Museum at Kitty Hawk, where the first airplane flight took place in 1903.

State Stats

Abbreviation: NC

Area: 53,821 square miles (139,396 km²)

Total Population (2000 Census): 8,049,313

Capital: Raleigh

Date of Statehood: Became the 12th state on November 21, 1789

Largest Cities (by population): Charlotte, Raleigh, Greensboro, Durham, Winston-Salem, Fayetteville

Flower: Dogwood

Tree: Longleaf pine

Bird: Cardinal

State Motto: "To Be, Rather Than to Seem"

Economy:
Agriculture – Cattle, hogs, milk, nursery stock, poultry and eggs, soybeans, tobacco
Industry – Bricks, chemical products, electrical equipment, furniture, machinery, textile goods, tobacco products, tourism

Famous North Carolinians

Howard Cosell
sportscaster

Roberta Flack
pop singer

Ava Gardner
actress

Dolley Payne Madison
first lady

Thelonious Monk
jazz musician

Edward R. Murrow
journalist

James K. Polk
11th president of the United States

Wright Brothers National Memorial

Fun Facts

- Fayetteville is the home of the nation's first miniature golf course.

- More sweet potatoes are grown in North Carolina than in any other state.

- In 1898, Pepsi-Cola was invented in New Bern.

- On March 7, 1914, in Fayetteville, baseball player Babe Ruth hit his first professional home run.

- Nationally popular Krispy Kreme doughnuts were first made in Winston-Salem.

- Virginia Dare, born in 1587 on Roanoke Island, was the first English baby to be born in America.

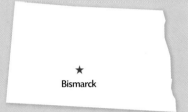

★
Bismarck

North Dakota was first explored by French-Canadians in 1738. The United States acquired most of the territory from France in 1803 as part of the Louisiana Purchase. The first permanent settlements were established in 1812 at Pembina by Irish and Scottish families. The area remained largely unsettled until the construction of the railroad in the 1870s and 1880s. Of all the states in the United States, North Dakota has the most farms—farmland covers 90 percent of the state. The Garrison Dam on the Missouri River provides irrigation to farms and generates electricity for the surrounding area.

State Stats

Abbreviation: ND

Area: 70,704 square miles (183,123 km²)

Total Population (2000 Census): 642,200

Capital: Bismarck

Date of Statehood: Became the 39th state on November 2, 1889

Largest Cities (by population): Fargo, Bismarck, Grand Forks, Minot, Mandan, West Fargo

Flower: Wild prairie rose

Tree: American elm

Bird: Western meadowlark

State Motto: "Liberty and Union, Now and Forever, One and Inseparable"

Economy:
Agriculture – Barley, cattle, milk, sugar beets, sunflowers, wheat
Industry – Food processing, machinery, mining, tourism

Famous North Dakotans

Elizabeth Bodine
humanitarian

Anne Carlsen
educator, advocate for people with disabilities

Angie Dickinson
actress

Phil Jackson
basketball player and coach

Louis L'Amour
author

Peggy Lee
jazz and pop singer

Eric Sevareid
television newscaster

Cowboys on the Range

Fun Facts

- Lewis and Clark first saw grizzly bears in North Dakota.

- Twelve full-scale dinosaurs can be found in Dickinson's Dakota Dinosaur Museum.

- Attempts to drop the word *North* from the state name were defeated by the state legislature in 1947 and 1989.

- The grave of Sitting Bull is preserved at the Sitting Bull Burial State Historic Site in Fort Yates.

- The world's largest hamburger, at 3,591 pounds (1,629 kg), was made in Rutland in 1982.

- In 1987, the North Dakota state legislature declared English the official state language.

OHIO The Buckeye State

★
Columbus

First explored by the French, the Ohio Territory came under British control in 1668. After the Revolutionary War, Ohio became part of the United States. In 1788, the first permanent settlement was established at Marietta, which became the capital of the entire Northwest Territory. By the 20th century, Ohio had become one of the leading industrial states in the United States. Everything from rubber to jet engines is manufactured in Ohio. The state's fertile farmlands produce corn, oats, and soybeans. Tourists flock to the Pro Football Hall of Fame in Canton and the Rock and Roll Hall of Fame in Cleveland.

State Stats

Abbreviation: OH

Area: 44,828 square miles (116,104 km²)

Total Population (2000 Census): 11,353,140

Capital: Columbus

Date of Statehood: Became the 17th state on March 1, 1803

Largest Cities (by population): Columbus, Cleveland, Cincinnati, Toledo, Akron, Dayton

Flower: Scarlet carnation

Tree: Ohio buckeye

Bird: Cardinal

State Motto: "With God, All Things Are Possible"

Economy:
Agriculture – Cattle, corn, dairy products, hogs, poultry and eggs, soybeans, tomatoes
Industry – Electrical equipment, fabricated metal products, food processing, machinery, transportation equipment

Famous Ohioans

Neil Armstrong
astronaut

Erma Bombeck
writer, humorist

Thomas Edison
inventor

Ulysses S. Grant
18th president of the United States

Toni Morrison
author

Steven Spielberg
film director, screenwriter

Gloria Steinem
women's rights activist

Ohio Roadside

Fun Facts

- Ohio is the birthplace of seven U.S. presidents: James Garfield, Ulysses S. Grant, Warren G. Harding, Benjamin Harrison, Rutherford B. Hayes, William McKinley, and William H. Taft.

- In 1852, Ohio became the first state to pass laws that protected working women.

- The Cincinnati Reds became the first professional baseball team in 1876.

- Neil Armstrong, from Wapakoneta, was the first person to walk on the moon.

- In 1879, Cleveland became the first city in the world to receive electric lights.

- John Glenn became the first American to orbit Earth on February 20, 1962.

State Flag

★ Oklahoma City

Spanish explorer Francisco Vásquez de Coronado traveled through Oklahoma in 1541. The territory fell into French hands and then became part of the United States in 1803, as a result of the Louisiana Purchase. April 22, 1889, was the first day homesteading was allowed in Oklahoma. On that day, 50,000 swarmed into the territory. Those who tried to beat the noon starting gun were called "Sooners," and they gave the state its nickname. In 1890, Oklahoma was divided into the Indian Territory and the Oklahoma Territory. Then in 1907, the two territories were combined to create the state of Oklahoma.

State Stats

Abbreviation: OK

Area: 69,903 square miles (181,049 km)

Total Population (2000 Census): 3,450,654

Capital: Oklahoma City

Date of Statehood: Became the 46th state on November 16, 1907

Largest Cities (by population): Oklahoma City, Tulsa, Norman, Lawton, Broken Arrow, Edmond

Flower: Mistletoe

Tree: Redbud

Bird: Scissor-tailed flycatcher

State Motto: "Labor Conquers All Things"

Economy:
Agriculture – Cattle, cotton, milk, poultry, wheat
Industry – Electrical equipment, food processing, machinery, rubber and plastic products, transportation equipment

Famous Oklahomans

Ralph Ellison
author

Jeane Kirkpatrick
diplomat

Wilma Mankiller
Cherokee chief

Mickey Mantle
baseball player

Patti Page
pop singer

Will Rogers
humorist

Maria Tallchief
dancer

Oklahoma City Skyline

Fun Facts

- The National Cowboy Hall of Fame is in Oklahoma City.

- The electric guitar, which would revolutionize guitar music, was invented by Bob Dunn of Beggs in 1935.

- The first radio station to broadcast from west of the Mississippi River was WKY Radio.

- A life-sized statue depicting a cattle drive, called "On the Chisholm Trail," was erected in Duncan in 1998.

- Got any change? The world's first parking meter was put in Oklahoma City in 1935.

- The tribal capital of the Cherokee Nation is Tahlequah.

State Flag

★ Salem

Both Spanish and English sailors are believed to have spotted the Oregon coast in the 1500s and 1600s. Then in 1778, Captain James Cook charted the coastline. In 1792, Captain Robert Gray discovered the Columbia River and claimed the Oregon Territory for the United States. In 1805, Meriwether Lewis and William Clark explored the area. For the next 40 years, disputes erupted between the British Hudson Bay Company and American settlers. Finally, in 1846, England gave up its claim to the region. Today, Oregon is known for its lumber and the great natural beauty of Crater Lake National Park.

State Stats

Abbreviation: OR

Area: 98,386 square miles (254,820 km²)

Total Population (2000 Census): 3,421,399

Capital: Salem

Date of Statehood: Became the 33rd state on February 14, 1859

Largest Cities (by population): Portland, Salem, Eugene, Gresham, Beaverton, Hillsboro

Flower: Oregon grape

Tree: Douglas fir

Bird: Western meadowlark

State Motto: "She Flies with Her Own Wings"

Economy:
Agriculture – Cattle, dairy products, fruits and nuts, nursery stock, vegetables, wheat
Industry – Food processing, lumber and wood products, machinery, paper products, scientific instruments, tourism

Famous Oregonians

Raymond Carver
author

Matt Groening
cartoonist

Mark Hatfield
U.S. senator

Joni Huntley
Olympic track athlete

Phyllis McGinley
poet

Linus Pauling
chemist

Jane Powell
pop singer, actress

Stone marker for the Oregon Trail

Fun Facts

- The world's largest collection of carousel horses is in Hood River's International Museum of Carousel Art.

- At depths of over 1,900 feet (580 m), Crater Lake is the deepest lake in the nation.

- Hells Canyon is the deepest river gorge in North America, dropping to 8,000 feet (2,438 m).

- The coast Douglas fir is the state's largest tree, sometimes rising 330 feet (100 m).

- The lighthouse considered to be the most often photographed in America is Lane County's Heceta Head Lighthouse.

- Scared of ghosts? Oregon has the most ghost towns of any state.

PENNSYLVANIA The Keystone State

Harrisburg
★

One of the most historically rich regions in the country, Pennsylvania was fought over by the Dutch, Swedes, and English in the early 1600s. The British took control in 1664 when they gained New York. Philadelphia was the seat of government for the young United States from 1776 to 1800. The Declaration of Independence was signed there in 1776, and the U.S. Constitution was written there in 1787. Valley Forge played a key role in the American Revolution, and the Battle of Gettysburg was a pivotal conflict of the Civil War. The mining of coal and ore, coupled with its 59,000 farms, forms the basis of present-day Pennsylvania's economy.

State Stats

Abbreviation: PA

Area: 46,058 square miles (119,290 km²)

Total Population (2000 Census): 12,281,054

Capital: Harrisburg

Date of Statehood: Became the second state on December 12, 1787

Largest Cities (by population): Philadelphia, Pittsburgh, Allentown, Erie, Upper Darby, Reading

Flower: Mountain laurel

Tree: Eastern hemlock

Bird: Ruffed grouse

State Motto: "Virtue, Liberty, and Independence"

Economy:
Agriculture – Cattle, dairy products, hay, hogs, mushrooms, nursery stock, poultry
Industry – Chemical products, electrical equipment, food processing, machinery, tourism

Famous Pennsylvanians

Louisa May Alcott
author

Rachel Carson
biologist, author

Bill Cosby
actor, comedian

Martha Graham
choreographer

Margaret Mead
anthropologist

James Stewart
actor

Honus Wagner
baseball player

John Barry Monument and Independence Hall

Fun Facts

- The first oil well in the United States was dug in Titusville in 1859.

- The most famous citizen of Punxsutawney is groundhog Punxsutawney Phil, who checks his shadow each February 2.

- Hershey is known as "the Chocolate Capital of the World."

- The first commercial radio broadcast in the United States originated in Pittsburgh on November 2, 1920, on station KDKA.

- The Little League Baseball World Series has been held in Williamsport each year since 1946.

- The Philadelphia Zoo, the first public zoo in the country, was opened in 1874.

RHODE ISLAND The Ocean State

Founded as a haven for religious freedom, Rhode Island gained a reputation as a place where freedom and rebellion thrived. Its colonists burned British ships shortly before the Revolutionary War. It refused to participate in the War of 1812. It is the smallest state in the United States.

State Stats

Abbreviation: RI

Area: 1,545 square miles (4,002 km²)

Total Population (2000 Census): 1,048,319

Capital: Providence

Date of Statehood: Became the 13th state on May 29, 1790

Largest Cities (by population): Providence, Warwick, Cranston, Pawtucket, East Providence, Woonsocket

Flower: Violet

Tree: Red maple

Bird: Rhode Island red

State Motto: "Hope"

Economy:
Agriculture – Dairy products, eggs, nursery stock, vegetables
Industry – Electrical equipment, fabricated metal products, jewelry, machinery, shipbuilding, tourism

Fun Facts

- Each year, the city of Newport hosts a jazz festival and a folk festival that draw crowds from around the world.

- The oldest schoolhouse in the country was put up in 1716. It is located in Portsmouth.

SOUTH CAROLINA The Palmetto State

The first South Carolina settlement was established by the British in 1670. South Carolina was the scene of many Revolutionary War battles. The state was the first to secede from the Union at the start of the Civil War, which began in 1861 when South Carolina troops fired on Fort Sumter.

State Stats

Abbreviation: SC

Area: 32,007 square miles (82,898 km²)

Total Population (2000 Census): 4,012,012

Capital: Columbia

Date of Statehood: Became the eighth state on May 23, 1788

Largest Cities (by population): Columbia, Charleston, North Charleston, Rock Hill, Greenville, Mount Pleasant

Flower: Yellow jessamine

Tree: Cabbage palmetto

Bird: Great Carolina wren

State Motto: "Prepared in Mind and Resources"

Economy:
Agriculture – Cattle, dairy products, hogs, poultry, soybeans, tobacco
Industry – Chemical products, machinery, paper products, textile goods, tourism

Fun Facts

- Myrtle Beach, on the South Carolina coast, has become a popular resort area in the last 25 years.

- The highest waterfall in the eastern United States is the Upper Whitewater Falls, which drops 411 feet (125 m) to the river below.

State Flag

★
Pierre

The French were the first Europeans in South Dakota. The United States acquired the territory as part of the Louisiana Purchase in 1803. The first permanent settlement, Fort Pierre, was established in 1817. In 1873, the railroad finally arrived in South Dakota. That, coupled with the discovery of gold in the Black Hills the following year, led to the mass settlement of the area. The state's most famous landmark is Mount Rushmore in the Black Hills. This monument to four U.S. presidents – George Washington, Thomas Jefferson, Abraham Lincoln, and Theodore Roosevelt – attracts thousands of visitors each year.

State Stats

Abbreviation: SD

Area: 77,121 square miles (199,743 km²)

Total Population (2000 Census): 754,844

Capital: Pierre

Date of Statehood: Became the 40th state on November 2, 1889

Largest Cities (by population): Sioux Falls, Rapid City, Aberdeen, Watertown, Brookings, Mitchell

Flower: Pasque

Tree: White spruce

Bird: Ring-necked pheasant

State Motto: "Under God the People Rule"

Economy:
Agriculture – Cattle, corn, hogs, milk, soybeans, wheat
Industry – Food processing, lumber and wood products, machinery, tourism

Famous South Dakotans

Sparky Anderson
baseball manager

Tom Brokaw
television newscaster

Crazy Horse
Sioux chief

Mary Hart
television host

Hubert H. Humphrey
U.S. vice president

Judith K. Meierhenry
South Dakota Supreme Court justice

Dorothy Provine
actress

Mount Rushmore

Fun Facts

- South Dakota is home to the Native American Sioux Nation.

- There is only one poisonous snake native to South Dakota—the prairie rattlesnake.

- Glimmering calcite crystals give the massive Jewel Cave its name.

- Many woolly mammoth bones were found still in their original resting place at the Mammoth Site of Hot Springs.

- The Mount Rushmore monument, begun in 1927, took 14 years to complete at a cost of $1 million.

- The country's highest point east of the Rocky Mountains is Harney Peak, at 7,242 feet (2,207 m).

TENNESSEE The Volunteer State

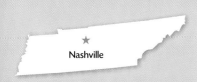

Nashville

Originally explored by the Spanish in the 1500s, Tennessee was claimed by both France and England in the 1600s. France finally took control of the area in 1763, after the French and Indian War. Although Tennessee joined the Confederacy during the Civil War, many people in the state supported the Union, and the region was the scene of many battles. Today, Tennessee is a major tobacco producer and a large provider of dairy products. The Tennessee Valley Authority operates a system of dams and reservoirs throughout the state. Tourists come to Tennessee to visit the beautiful Great Smoky Mountains National Park.

State Stats

Abbreviation: TN

Area: 42,146 square miles (109,158 km²)

Total Population (2000 Census): 5,689,283

Capital: Nashville

Date of Statehood: Became the 16th state on June 1, 1796

Largest Cities (by population): Memphis, Nashville, Knoxville, Chattanooga, Clarksville, Murfreesboro

Flower: Iris

Tree: Yellow poplar

Bird: Mockingbird

State Motto: "Agriculture and Commerce"

Economy:
Agriculture – Cattle, cotton, dairy products, hogs, livestock and livestock products, soybeans, tobacco
Industry – Chemicals, rubber and plastic products, transportation equipment

Famous Tennesseans

James Agee
writer, poet

Hattie Caraway
first woman elected to the U.S. Senate

Davy Crockett
frontiersman

Aretha Franklin
pop and soul singer

Albert Gore Jr.
U.S. vice president

Wilma Rudolph
Olympic track athlete

Cybill Shepherd
actress

Battlefield in Chattanooga

Fun Facts

- Shelby County has more horses per capita than any other U.S. county.

- The first female U.S. senator was Hattie Caraway of Bakersfield in 1931.

- During the War of 1812, Tennessee gained its nickname, "the Volunteer State," when a group of volunteer soldiers from the state fought in the Battle of New Orleans.

- Too much mining in the Copper Basin of Tennessee has created a bleak landscape that can be spotted from space.

- There are over 3,800 known caves in Tenessee.

- More people visit Elvis Presley's home, Graceland, in Memphis, than any other U.S. house, except for the White House.

TEXAS
The Lone Star State

State Flag

★ Austin

After early Spanish and French settlement, Americans began to settle Texas in 1821, led by Stephen Austin. At that time, Texas was controlled by Mexico. In 1836, a war broke out between American settlers in Texas and the Mexican government. The famous battles of the Alamo and San Jacinto resulted in Texas becoming a separate country, with Sam Houston as president. In 1845, Texas became a U.S. state. Border disputes resulted in the Mexican-American War from 1846 to 1848. The largest state in the lower forty-eight, Texas is rich in natural resources, Today, the Alamo is the state's most popular historic site.

State Stats

Abbreviation: TX

Area: 268,601 square miles (695,677 km²)

Total Population (2000 Census): 20,851,820

Capital: Austin

Date of Statehood: Became the 28th state on December 29, 1845

Largest Cities (by population): Houston, San Antonio, Dallas, Austin, Fort Worth, El Paso

Flower: Bluebonnet

Tree: Pecan

Bird: Mockingbird

State Motto: "Friendship"

Economy:
Agriculture – Cattle, corn, cotton, dairy products, nursery stock, poultry, sorghum, wheat
Industry – Chemical products, electrical equipment, food processing, machinery, mining, petroleum and natural gas, tourism

Famous Texans

Carol Burnett
actress, comedienne

Dwight D. Eisenhower
34th president of the United States

Jack Johnson
boxer

Lyndon B. Johnson
36th president of the United States

Janis Joplin
blues and rock singer

Sandra Day O'Connor
Supreme Court justice

Babe Didrikson Zaharias
Olympic track athlete, golfer

Texas Oil Pump

Fun Facts

- Six different flags have been used by Texas throughout its history—the flags of Spain, France, Mexico, the Republic of Texas, the Confederate States, and the United States.

- The Alamo in San Antonio is the site of one of the most famous battles in U.S. history.

- Texas is so big that El Paso is closer to Needles, California, than it is to Dallas.

- A Texas ranch called the King Ranch is bigger than all of Rhode Island.

- A 1,500-year-old tree grows near Fulton. This coastal live oak is the oldest tree in the state.

- During the course of the turbulent year 1836, five different places were temporary capitals of Texas.

UTAH The Beehive State

★ Salt Lake City

The first Europeans to explore Utah were Franciscan friars from Spain in 1776. In 1824, American frontiersman Jim Bridger discovered the Great Salt Lake. Fleeing religious persecution in the East and the Midwest, the Mormons arrived in 1847 and began building Salt Lake City. The United States acquired Utah at the end of the Mexican-American War in 1848. In 1869, the first transcontinental railroad was completed in Utah, which helped open up the West. Today, agriculture and mining make up a large part of Utah's economy, and visitors enjoy the natural beauty of Bryce Canyon and Zion National Parks.

State Stats

Abbreviation: UT

Area: 84,904 square miles (219,901 km²)

Total Population (2000 Census): 2,233,169

Capital: Salt Lake City

Date of Statehood: Became the 45th state on January 4, 1896

Largest Cities (by population): Salt Lake City, West Valley City, Provo, Sandy, Orem, West Jordan

Flower: Sego lily

Tree: Blue spruce

Bird: Common American gull

State Motto: "Industry"

Economy:
Agriculture – Cattle, dairy products, hay, turkeys
Industry – Aerospace, electrical equipment, food processing, machinery, mining, tourism

Famous Utahns

Roseanne Barr
actress, comedienne

Butch Cassidy
outlaw

Avard Fairbanks
sculptor

Philo Farnsworth
inventor

Jake Garn
U.S. senator

Ivy Baker Priest
U.S. treasurer

Virginia Sorensen
author

Arches National Park

Fun Facts

- Utah takes its name from the native Ute tribe. *Ute* means "people of the mountains."

- The Great Salt Lake stretches over 2,100 square miles (5,440 km²).

- On May 10, 1869, the first transcontinental railroad in the United States was finished. The Central Pacific and Union Pacific Railroads met at Promontory.

- It took builders 40 years to construct the Mormon Temple in Salt Lake City.

- The first department store in the United States opened in Utah in the late 1800s.

- Five national parks are situated within Utah's borders—Arches, Bryce, Canyonlands, Capitol Reef, and Zion.

VERMONT The Green Mountain State

State Flag

Montpelier

France established the first Vermont settlement in 1666. The British gained control of the region in 1763 after the French and Indian War. Originally organized to drive settlers from New York out of Vermont, the Green Mountain Boys, led by Ethan Allen, captured Fort Ticonderoga from the British in the early part of the Revolutionary War, becoming instant heroes. Vermont, which abolished slavery in 1777, has always had a reputation as a place that cherishes freedom. Today, tourists enjoy world-class skiing and visiting the beautiful Green Mountain National Forest.

State Stats

Abbreviation: VT

Area: 9,615 square miles (24,903 km²)

Total Population (2000 Census): 608,827

Capital: Montpelier

Date of Statehood: Became the 14th state on March 4, 1791

Largest Cities (by population): Burlington, Essex, Colchester, Rutland, South Burlington, Bennington

Flower: Red clover

Tree: Sugar maple

Bird: Hermit thrush

State Motto: "Freedom and Unity"

Economy:
Agriculture – Apples, cattle, dairy products, hay, maple products
Industry – Electrical components, fabricated metal products, paper products, printing and publishing, tourism

Famous Vermonters

Chester A. Arthur
21st president of the United States

Myra Colby Bradwell
lawyer, editor

Calvin Coolidge
30th president of the United States

John Deere
blacksmith, inventor, manufacturer

Elisha Otis
inventor

Patty Sheehan
golfer

Jody Williams
Nobel Peace Prize winner

Covered Bridge in Winter

Fun Facts

- The state capital with the smallest population is Montpelier, with less than 9,000 residents.

- Ben and Jerry's Ice Cream began in Vermont.

- Calvin Coolidge, born in Plymouth in 1872, was the only U.S. president who was born on July 4.

- In the 1890s, writer Rudyard Kipling invented the game of snow golf while living in Vermont.

- Vermont has more dairy cows per person than any other state in the nation.

- More maple syrup is made in Montpelier than in any other town in the country.

VIRGINIA The Old Dominion State

State Flag

Richmond ★

Virginia has played a major role in the history of the United States. Jamestown, founded in 1607, was the first permanent English settlement in North America. Slavery was introduced to the continent in Virginia in 1619. The British surrendered at Yorktown in 1781 to end the Revolutionary War, and the Confederates surrendered at Appomattox in 1865 to end the Civil War. Today, Virginia is one of the major coal producers in the United States. Agriculture, including the growing of tobacco, is also a large part of the state's economy. Tourists enjoy visiting George Washington's home, Mount Vernon, and Thomas Jefferson's home, Monticello.

State Stats

Abbreviation: VA

Area: 42,769 square miles (110,772 km²)

Total Population (2000 Census): 7,078,515

Capital: Richmond

Date of Statehood: Became the 10th state on June 25, 1788

Largest Cities (by population): Virginia Beach, Norfolk, Chesapeake, Richmond, Newport News, Hampton

Flower: Dogwood

Tree: Flowering dogwood

Bird: Cardinal

State Motto: "Thus Always to Tyrants"

Economy:
Agriculture – Cattle, dairy products, hogs, poultry, soybeans, tobacco
Industry – Chemicals, electrical equipment, food processing, printing, textiles, transportation equipment

Famous Virginians

Arthur Ashe
tennis player

Pearl Bailey
pop singer

Willa Cather
author

Ella Fitzgerald
jazz singer

Robert E. Lee
Confederate general

Shirley MacLaine
actress

Booker T. Washington
educator

Thomas Jefferson's Monticello

Fun Facts

- Kentucky and West Virginia are both made up of land that was once part of Virginia.

- Virginia has produced eight U.S. presidents, including Thomas Jefferson, James Madison, and George Washington.

- More than 2,200 of the 4,000 battles of the Civil War took place in Virginia.

- Virginia farmers produced the first peanuts ever grown in the country.

- The largest office building in the world is the Pentagon in Arlington, Virginia.

- About one-quarter of all people who work in Virginia are employed by the U.S. government.

WASHINGTON The Evergreen State

State Flag

Washington was visited by the Spanish and the British and explored as part of the Lewis and Clark expedition in the early 1800s. American and British settlers almost went to war against each other in the 1840s, but the dispute was settled by the Oregon Treaty in 1849. Today, Washington is a major producer of lumber and has over 1,000 dams.

State Stats

Abbreviation: WA

Area: 71,303 square miles (184,675 km²)

Total Population (2000 Census): 5,894,121

Capital: Olympia

Date of Statehood: Became the 42nd state on November 11, 1889

Largest Cities (by population): Seattle, Tacoma, Spokane, Vancouver, Bellevue, Everett

Flower: Pink rhododendron

Tree: Western hemlock

Bird: Willow goldfinch

State Motto: "By and By"

Economy:
Agriculture – Apples, cattle, dairy products, nursery stock, potatoes, seafood, wheat
Industry – Aerospace, chemical products, food processing, lumber and wood products, paper products, software development, tourism

★ Olympia

Fun Facts

- More apples come from Washington than from any other state.

- The first soft ice cream in the world came from a Dairy Queen in Olympia.

WEST VIRGINIA The Mountain State

State Flag

West Virginia was part of Virginia from 1609 until 1863. In 1861, when Virginia seceded from the Union, delegates from 40 western counties who opposed secession formed their own government. They were granted independent statehood two years later. Today, West Virginia produces about 15 percent of the coal in the United States.

State Stats

Abbreviation: WV

Area: 24,231 square miles (62,758 km²)

Total Population (2000 Census): 1,808,344

Capital: Charleston

Date of Statehood: Became the 35th state on June 20, 1863

Largest Cities (by population): Charleston, Huntington, Parkersburg, Wheeling, Morgantown, Weirton

Flower: Rhododendron

Tree: Sugar maple

Bird: Cardinal

State Motto: "Mountaineers Are Always Free"

Economy:
Agriculture – Apples, cattle, dairy products, poultry
Industry – Chemical products, mining, stone, clay, and glass products, tourism

Charleston ★

Fun Facts

- West Virginia produces 15 percent of all the coal in the United States.

- The Native American burial mound in Moundsville is one of the largest in North America.

WISCONSIN The Badger State

Madison ★

The first Europeans in Wisconsin were French explorers in 1634. England gained control in 1763, after the French and Indian War, and the United States took over in 1783, after the Revolutionary War. Wisconsin became a separate territory in 1836. Today, it is well known for its dairy products. The state was the first to provide pensions for the blind in 1907, aid to dependent children in 1913, and help for senior citizens in 1925. Wisconsin was also the first state to offer unemployment and workers' compensation, both in the 1930s. The state has over 14,000 lakes that are enjoyed by residents and visitors alike.

State Stats

Abbreviation: WI

Area: 65,503 square miles (169,653 km²)

Total Population (2000 Census): 5,363,675

Capital: Madison

Date of Statehood: Became the 30th state on May 29, 1848

Largest Cities (by population): Milwaukee, Madison, Green Bay, Kenosha, Racine, Appleton

Flower: Wood violet

Tree: Sugar maple

Bird: Robin

State Motto: "Forward"

Economy:
Agriculture – Cattle, cheese and other dairy products, corn, cranberries, hogs, vegetables
Industry – Electrical equipment, fabricated metal products, food processing, machinery, paper products, tourism

Famous Wisconsinites

Carrie Catt
women's rights activist

Harry Houdini
magician

Georgia O'Keeffe
artist

Hildegarde Loretta Sell
cabaret singer

Orson Welles
actor, producer, filmmaker

Laura Ingalls Wilder
author

Frank Lloyd Wright
architect

Cows Graze on the Farm

Fun Facts

- More milk is produced in Wisconsin than in any other state.

- Over 2,300 types of mustard can be found at the Mustard Museum in Mount Horeb.

- The Harley-Davidson Motor Company is headquartered in Milwaukee.

- Wisconsin has 7,446 rivers and streams, which have a total combined length of 26,767 miles (43,608 km) – enough to go around the entire Earth!

- The world-famous Ringling Brothers Circus began in 1884 in Baraboo.

- Eagle River is known for the huge number of snowmobilers who take advantage of the snowfall there each winter.

State Flag

Cheyenne ★

The United States acquired Wyoming from France in 1803 as part of the Louisiana Purchase. In 1807, fur trapper John Colter explored the Yellowstone area and returned home with word of the amazing geysers and hot springs there. Fort Laramie, the first permanent trading post in Wyoming, was established in 1834. In 1869, Wyoming women became the first in the nation to get the right to vote. In 1925, the people of Wyoming elected the first woman governor in the United States. Wyoming's natural beauty is one of its great assets. Each year, visitors flock to Yellowstone and Grand Teton National Parks.

State Stats

Abbreviation: WY

Area: 97,818 square miles (253,349 km²)

Total Population (2000 Census): 493,782

Capital: Cheyenne

Date of Statehood: Became the 44th state on July 10, 1890

Largest Cities (by population): Cheyenne, Casper, Laramie, Gillette, Rock Springs, Sheridan

Flower: Indian paintbrush

Tree: Cottonwood

Bird: Western meadowlark

State Motto: "Equal Rights"

Economy:
Agriculture – Cattle, hay, sheep, sugar beets, wheat
Industry – Chemical products, lumber and wood products, machinery, mining, printing and publishing, tourism

Famous Wyomingites

June Etta Downey
psychologist, educator

Curt Gowdy
sportscaster

Isabel Jewell
actress

Patricia MacLachlan
children's author

Jackson Pollock
artist

Alan K. Simpson
U.S. senator

Washakie
Shoshone chief

Old Faithful

Fun Facts

- In Wyoming in 1925, Nellie Tayloe Ross became the first woman to be elected governor in the United States.

- Fewer people live in Wyoming than in any other state.

- The Jackson Hole Ski Area has the longest continuous vertical run of any ski area in the United States, at 4,139 feet (1,262 m).

- Yellowstone became the first official national park in the nation in 1872.

- The Black Thunder Mine near Wright is the biggest coal mine in the country.

- World-famous JCPenney stores originated in the town of Kemmerer.